The AMERICAN

CONGRESS

MESSNER BOOKS BY ANN E. WEISS

THE AMERICAN CONGRESS

THE AMERICAN PRESIDENCY

SAVE THE MUSTANGS:
    How a Federal Law Is Passed

WE WILL BE HEARD:
    Dissent in the United States

FIVE ROADS TO THE WHITE
    HOUSE

THE VITAMIN PUZZLE
    (with Malcolm E. Weiss)

The AMERICAN
CONGRESS

by ANN E. WEISS

Illustrated with photographs and engravings

JULIAN MESSNER New York

Design by Ruth Bornschlegel

Library of Congress Cataloging in Publication Data

Weiss, Ann E   1943–
    The American Congress.

    Includes index.
    SUMMARY: Discusses the history and functions of the
legislative branch of our government.
    1.   United States.   Congress—Juvenile literature.
[1.   United States.   Congress]   I.   Title.
JK1064.W44   328.73   77-21818
ISBN 0-671-32845-X

ACKNOWLEDGMENTS

I want to thank the staffs of Senator Edmund S. Muskie and Representative David F. Emery for their assistance in helping to find the answers to my many questions.

PHOTO CREDITS

CONTENTS

Note to the Reader

As you read this book, you'll see that we call a member of Congress a Congressman. There are two reasons for this. First, there were no women in Congress until 1917. Since then, however, women have served side by side with men in both houses of Congress. Yet to express this over and over would mean having sentences like this: A Congressman or woman chooses for his or her staff people who can help him or her in his or her work. That's a pretty silly sentence! So just remember: in talking about the modern Congress, "Congressman" means "Congresswoman," too.

A.E.W.

Visitors stroll through the Hall of Statuary in the United States Capitol building. Statues of outstanding leaders from each state are displayed here.

Chapter 1

CAPITOL HILL–AND BEYOND

A small hill rises in the center of Washington, D.C.. It is called Capitol Hill. Upon it is the building that lies at the heart of our federal government—the United States Capitol.

The Capitol is a beautiful building of gleaming white marble. It is five stories high and takes up three and a half acres of ground. Columns and statues decorate its front wall, or facade. Atop its three-hundred-foot-high dome stands the Statue of Freedom.

Inside, the Capitol is equally beautiful. Heavy bronze doors open onto the Great Rotunda, or round hall, nearly one hundred feet across. Paintings of Revolutionary War scenes cover the walls. Beyond the Great Rotunda are the North Small Rotunda, the South Small Rotunda and the Hall of Statuary.

The importance of the Capitol, however, does not lie in its size, nor in its statues or paintings. It lies in the two rooms on either side of the Great Rotunda.

In these rooms, voices have been raised in angry argument. Great speeches have moved listeners deeply. Soft-voiced discussions have changed the course of our country's history. Into these rooms have come the hopes and fears and wishes of the American people. From these rooms have gone the federal laws under which all Americans live. These are the rooms in which the two houses of the United States Congress—the Senate and the House of Representatives —have met for over one hundred and fifteen years.

To many Americans, these meetings *are* Congress. After all, the word "Congress" means meeting. But the members of Congress know that Congress is more than meetings. Congress reaches beyond the Capitol.

Stretching out from the Capitol like the spokes of a wheel are the streets and avenues of the city of Washington. Closest to the Capitol are the buildings in which Senators and Representatives have their offices. In these offices, the men and women on the staff of each member of Congress are hard at work. They are writing speeches, researching facts, answering questions. These staffs are also part of Congress.

Congress is still more. "Congress is the people," said Representative Thaddeus Stevens of Pennsylvania more than a century ago. And that's exactly what Congress is supposed to be. Of all the parts of the federal government, Congress is closest to all the people of the United States of America.

The President lives apart from ordinary citizens. He travels in a private plane or helicopter or

The Capitol and its tree-filled grounds dominate the city of Washington. Surrounding the Capitol are the office buildings where Senators and Representatives do much of their work. In the distance are the Washington Monument and the Potomac River.

limousine. He is surrounded by Secret Service men whose job is to protect him from harm.

The men and women who advise the President and who work with him are even further from the people. They are chosen for office by the President, not by the voters. Even their names are unfamiliar to most of us.

But Congressmen and women are not so distant from us. They cannot be. Members of the House of Representatives hold office for only two years at a time, Senators for six years. If they want to return to Congress, they must go back to the voters and ask to be re-elected. They must tell us what they have done for us in Congress. They must convince us that they have our interests at heart. If they do not, if they move too far away from those of us who elected them, they will lose our votes. We may send others to Congress.

But Senators and Representatives go back to the people more often than every sixth year or every other year. Each Congressman has a home and an office in his own state. He goes to picnics and barbeques, attends suppers, parties, and meetings in order to chat with old friends and to make new ones.

Such activities are supposed to be a way of making sure that members of Congress remain part of "the people." They're supposed to keep a Congressman in touch with his constituents—the people who elected him to office.

Members of Congress try to stay in touch with their constituents—the men and women who elected them to office. One way they do that is by taking part in parades. They also make speeches and meet with voters in smaller groups.

Are the members of Congress in touch with the people? Many Americans don't think so. They believe that too many Congressmen and women are out of touch with Americans. They say that Congress is not doing all it should for the American people.

Criticism like this is not new. Americans have always found fault with Congress. One of the first to do so was the "father of his country," George Washington.

Chapter 2

A NEW START

It was, thought George Washington, "absolute absurdity and madness." The General's quill pen spluttered furiously across the paper. "What a triumph for our enemies," he wrote, "to find we are incapable of governing ourselves."

Washington wrote these words to a friend in 1786. Just three years before, he had led the rebellious American colonists to victory over their English rulers. Now the United States was an independent country.

What bothered Washington was that the young United States still did not have a strong national government of its own. The country's only government was the Congress. And, Washington declared, there was "a want of power in Congress."

The American Congress had lacked power since its beginning in 1774. However, at first, its weakness was not so easily seen. During the Revolution, the thirteen states had shared a single aim: to become independent of England. Members of Congress from each state agreed that they must work together to win their country's freedom.

But when the war ended, so did most of the cooperation. Each Congressman wanted Congress to pass laws to benefit his own state. Most Congressmen voted against anything that would help another state.

Furthermore, each state had just one vote in Congress. Yet each state could send several men to represent it in Congress. Often it took the representatives from each state a long time to agree among themselves how to vote. As a result, Congress produced many arguments, and few laws.

Still another problem was that although Congress had the power to pass laws, it did not have the power to make people pay taxes. Without money from taxes, Congress could not pay for roads, bridges, or mail service. It couldn't even afford an army or a navy. Without good roads, Americans found travel slow and tiring. Trade was difficult. Mail delivery was uncertain. The lack of an army or a navy meant that the United States was at the mercy of foreign countries. No wonder George Washington thought the situation absurd and mad!

Washington was not the only one who felt this way. By 1787, he and other Americans were so worried that they decided to try to strengthen Congress. They met together for a Constitutional Convention

The summer of 1787 was hot in Philadelphia. The arguments of the delegates to the Constitutional Convention were hot, too! But compromises were reached, and the Constitution was written by fall. In this old drawing, George Washington presides over a meeting of the convention.

in Philadelphia, Pennsylvania, on the second Monday in May of that year.

Almost at once, the men realized that giving Congress a few new powers would not be enough to save the country. So instead, they began to make plans for a different kind of government. During the summer, they wrote a Constitution, setting down rules for the new government.

Deciding on the rules was no easy task. Some members of this Constitutional Convention argued for a strong federal government that could force the separate states to obey its laws. But others protested. The United States had just won its rebellion against the strong English government, they pointed out. What was the sense of substituting a strong American government for a strong English one?

Days passed and the argument grew fiercer. Tempers flared. One day, a convention member suggested that everyone give up and go home. Luckily the other delegates did not take his advice. Sometimes when the tension was greatest, Benjamin Franklin rose to tell a joke or a funny story. His good humor helped smooth over the worst arguments.

Then, at the end of May, the delegates reached an agreement. They decided to write a Constitution that provided for a strong federal government. But they divided that government into three separate parts, or branches. The *legislative* branch—the Congress—makes the laws. The *executive* branch—the President—manages the running of the government. The *judicial* branch includes the courts where lawbreakers may be brought to trial.

These three branches are supposed to balance each other. Each branch has certain definite powers. But under the Constitution, no one branch may seize all the power to run the country. If one branch tries to do so, either of the other branches has the right to check, or put a stop to, its growing strength. This system of government is called "checks and balances."

How do checks and balances work? Suppose the President wants a new law. He must ask Congress to vote for it. Congress may, or may not, do as the President wishes.

Or suppose Congress has its own idea for a new law. The idea is written up as a *bill*, which Congress may pass. Once passed, the bill is called an *act*. Congress sends its act to the President. If the President likes it, he signs it into law. Then he must make sure the *law* is obeyed. If anyone breaks it, that person is tried in a court.

What if the President does not like the act? He can refuse to sign it into law. This is called a *veto*. The President sends a vetoed act back to Congress. If two-thirds of the members of each house of Congress vote to pass the act again, it becomes law without the President's consent.

The Constitution mentions other ways in which the branches of government are to check and balance each other. The President can choose the men and women he wants for many government jobs. But the Senate must approve his choices. The President can work out treaty agreements with other nations, but the Senate must agree to those treaties. In wartime, the President is Commander-in-Chief of the country's armed forces. Yet according to the Constitution, only Congress can declare war.

Congress can even play a part in electing a President. If an election is so close that no one is the winner, the House of Representatives steps in. The House holds a Presidential election in which each state has one vote. The last President elected by the House was John Quincy Adams, in 1824.

The power to *impeach* is another checking power of Congress. Any official of the United States government, including the President, can be impeached, or accused of wrong-doing in office, by the House. An impeached official then goes on trial in the Senate. If two-thirds of the Senators vote to find him guilty, he must leave office.

Congress is also checked by the people. One way we do so is by voting for the men and women who represent us there. Another is in the way we amend, or change, the Constitution. A Constitutional amendment must be passed by two-thirds of the members of the House and two-thirds of the members of the Senate. Then it goes to the legislature of each state. If thirty-eight of the fifty legislatures approve the amendment within seven years, it becomes part of the Constitution.

When the members of the Constitutional Convention agreed to a system of checks and balances, they were well on their way to setting up the new government. But more arguments lay ahead of them. Many had to do with Congress.

The worst disagreement was over how many Congressmen each state should have. The delegates from states with large populations, like Virginia and Massachusetts, argued that the more people a state had, the more Congressmen it should have. Delegates from the small states thought this plan unfair. It meant their states would have little voice in Congress. Every state should have an equal voice, and an equal number of Congressmen, they said.

Finally, the delegates came up with a compromise. They divided Congress into two houses—the Senate and the House of Representatives. Each state, big and small, has two Senators. But membership in the House of Representatives is based on population. The more people a state has, the more Representatives it sends to Congress. Each state is divided into one or more *Congressional districts*. Every district is supposed to have the same number of people as every other district. And every district elects one Representative.

Now that the big battle about Congress was over, the delegates turned their attention to details. They decided that the Vice-president of the United States should act as President of the Senate. That means the Vice-president runs the Senate when it is in session. He does not vote in the Senate though, except to break a tie vote.

The delegates left it up to each house of Congress to choose all its other officers and to write its own rules. They agreed to permit each house to punish its own members for bad conduct. They decided that members of Congress should receive a salary, and that Congress itself should decide on the amount of that salary. Today, a Congressman gets $57,500 a year. In addition, he receives allowances, or extra money, for office staffs and supplies, travel, and other expenses. He has special privileges, too, such as the right to send up to 40,000 pieces of business mail a month, free.

The delegates wanted to make sure that the new Congress would remain active in the nation's affairs. So they added a provision that Congress must meet at least once every year. And they wanted the people to know what their Congress was doing. They agreed that both houses should keep journals of their daily activities. These journals—now called the Congressional Record—are published regularly. Anyone can receive copies of the Congressional Record by asking

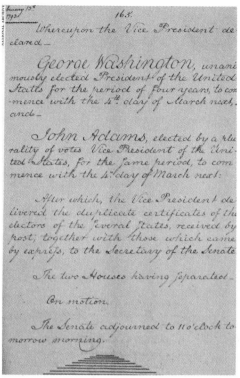

This is a page from the Senate Journal. The Constitution says Congress must keep a written account of its actions. Today, that account is called the Congressional Record.

his or her Congressman or woman.

All these rules about Congress are set down in Article I of the Constitution. Article I also includes a list of the powers of Congress. They are:

• To collect taxes
• To borrow money when the government needs it
• To make rules for trade between states and between the United States and other countries
• To coin money
• To set up a postal system
• To set up a system of courts (except for the Su-

preme Court, the nation's highest court, which is established in the Constitution)

• To declare war, raise and support an army and navy, and to call out the militia in times of emergency

• To make all the laws necessary to carry out these duties

Article I also includes a list of things Congress *cannot* do. For example, Congress cannot make laws that help one state's trade and hurt another's. Nor can it pass any law to punish anyone for doing something that was not a crime at the time the person did it. The delegates added such rules to protect the rights of American citizens.

Writing the Constitution took the whole summer. The delegates had to outline the powers and duties of the executive and judicial branches as carefully as they had those of the legislative branch. It was the middle of September, 1787, before they finished their work.

Now it was up to the states. Nine of the thirteen would have to ratify, or agree to, the Constitution before it could go into effect. The first state to ratify was Delaware, in December, 1787. The ninth was New Hampshire, on June 21, 1788.

The final step in setting up the new government was to hold elections—for President and for Congress—and to pick a date for the Constitution to become official. The date chosen was March 4, 1789.

Chapter 3

THE HOUSE OF REPRESENTATIVES

March 4, 1789 was also to have been the opening day for the First Congress of the United States. Already, the newly elected Senators and Representatives were arriving in New York. Most of them had found an opportunity to visit the old City Hall on Wall Street. City Hall, redecorated and renamed Federal Hall, was to be the new Congress's first home. Congress did not move to Washington, D.C., the permanent capital, until 1800.

Although Federal Hall was ready for Congress by March 4, Congress was not yet ready to open officially. It was nearly a month before either house reached a *quorum*. Each house must have a quorum—the presence of at least half its members—in order to hold official meetings. The Senate had no quorum until April 5. By then, the members of the House had been in session for four days. The Representatives had reached their quorum on April 1.

Congress' first home was Federal Hall, New York City's former City Hall. George Washington took the oath of office as the country's first President on the balcony. In 1790, Congress moved to Philadelphia, and in 1800, to Washington, D.C., the permanent capital.

What were they like, the sixty-five members of the first House? Elias Boudinot was a New Jersey lawyer, and a powerful speaker who could move his listeners to tears. Frederick Muhlenberg of Pennsylvania was a large, solemn man of German descent. Virginia's slight, short James Madison was known for his patient leadership. Madison had helped write the Constitution, and in 1809, he would become the fourth President of the United States. Fisher Ames of Massachusetts was an enthusiastic young bachelor who fretted aloud when he thought the House was moving too slowly. But patient or fretful, solemn or eloquent, all the Representatives had certain things in common. All were men. All were white. All were well-to-do.

Why? The Constitution did not say that a Representative must be twenty-five years old or older. He must have been a United States citizen for at least seven years. He must live in the state from which he is elected. He can be re-elected any number of times. There are no constitutional requirements about a Representative's education, job, color, or wealth.

But in 1789, most people took it for granted that only white men might be elected to Congress. In most states, white men were the only people allowed to vote. Blacks, whether slave or free, could not vote. In New Jersey, women could vote if they were wealthy. Other states did not give women the vote at all, and within twenty years, New Jersey women had lost it, too. Most states had laws that kept a man from voting unless he owned property—fifty acres of land, perhaps, or several hundred dollars. In some states, only members of Protestant churches could vote. New

Hampshire did not give the vote to Catholics until 1851.

The right to vote and serve in Congress came still more slowly to women and Blacks. Blacks got the vote in 1870, five years after slavery was outlawed. The first black Representative, Joseph Rainy of South

For 80 years, only white men served in Congress. Not until slavery was outlawed in this country were Blacks elected to Congress. The first black Senator and Representatives posed for this picture in 1872: (Back) Robert C. DeLarge of South Carolina and Jefferson H. Long of Georgia. (Front) Senator H. R. Revels of Mississippi, Benjamin S. Turner of Alabama, Josiah T. Walls of Florida, Joseph H. Rainy of South Carolina and R. Brown Elliot of South Carolina.

Carolina, was elected that year. The first Congress-woman, Jeanette Rankin of Montana, was elected in 1917. In Montana, women had been voting since 1914. In 1920, the Constitution was changed to give the vote to all American women.

But back in 1789, the idea that women or Blacks

It took women even longer than Blacks to get into Congress. The first Congresswoman, Jeanette Rankin of Montana, was elected twice: in 1917 and in 1941.

Frederick Muhlenberg of Pennsylvania was the first Speaker of the House of Representatives. He served as Speaker from 1789 to 1795.

would ever belong to Congress would have astonished most Representatives. Anyway, they were too busy to waste time thinking of such nonsense. As soon as the House officially opened, its members got down to work. At once, they chose Frederick Muhlenberg to be Speaker of the House. As Speaker, Muhlenberg was in charge of running House meetings. He had to call each meeting to order and recognize, or call on, Representatives who wished to speak.

The Representatives also chose someone to keep track of their business—to be a kind of secretary of the House. This person was the Clerk. Unlike the Speaker, the Clerk was not a member of the House. The Representatives chose other officers as well. They appointed a doorkeeper to guard against unwelcome visitors. They selected a sergeant-at-arms, whose job it was to round up members for a quorum.

The Representatives also needed rules to follow during their meetings. To write them, the Speaker appointed a Rules Committee.

As soon as it had rules and officers, the House was ready to begin making laws. The first major bill the Representatives considered was one to place a tax on goods shipped into the United States from other lands. This bill, like all bills introduced in Congress, had to be passed by both the House and the Senate before it could go to the President for his signature or veto.

Congress passed the first tax bill quickly, and President Washington signed it into law in July. By then, the Representatives were discussing other bills. At the same time, they were working out ways of doing business among themselves and between the House and the Senate.

For instance, members of the House realized that no single Representative had the time to learn all the details of all the bills that would be introduced in the House. Yet each Representative ought to know as much as possible about every bill he would have to vote on. So the Representatives set up a committee system.

As each bill was introduced in the House, the Speaker sent it to a committee. Committee members studied the bill and reported back to the House whether they thought it should pass. That meant each Representative had to learn the details of only a few bills. He could depend on members of other committees to inform him about other bills.

But there was a drawback to naming a separate committee to examine each bill. Before long, there were three hundred and fifty House committees! This was too many, and the Representatives agreed to establish just four standing, or permanent, committees.

As the years went by, the number of committees grew. Today, there are twenty-two standing committees in the House. In addition, there are a hundred and forty-seven smaller subcommittees.

Each committee deals with certain kinds of bills. The Ways and Means Committee, for example, examines all tax bills. Its members hold hearings to which they invite tax experts. Members of the public who will have to pay any new taxes may be invited, too.

The Representatives on the committee listen as citizens and experts discuss the good and bad points of each bill. They ask these witnesses questions. Then the committee members decide what to do about each bill. They may amend the bill slightly by making small changes in it. They may rewrite it completely before sending it back to the full membership of the House for a vote. Or they may "kill" a bill by refusing to send it back to the House at all.

Committees have another duty: investigation. The first Congressional investigation was carried out by a House committee in 1792. Its purpose: to learn why nine hundred United States Army soldiers had been killed by Indians in Ohio a few months earlier. The committee members wanted to know whether an officer's carelessness had allowed the Indians to take his men by surprise. They did not come up with a definite answer. But their investigation showed that Congress was willing to be responsible for checking up on the activities of other parts of the federal government.

Another kind of committee is the conference committee. Conference committees are joint House-Senate committees. They give Senators and Representatives a chance to work out disagreements between the two houses.

What sort of disagreements? It didn't take Congressmen long to discover that the House and Senate often passed bills that were very similar, but not exactly the same. A House bill might call for building ten new forts in the West. A Senate bill might call for building twelve forts. To get their bills to agree, the two houses could send them to a conference committee.

At the conference committee meeting, several Senators and Representatives would try to compromise on the number of new forts—perhaps eleven in this case. After reaching an agreement, they would rewrite the bills and send them back to the House and Senate. Now, each house could vote on exactly the same bill.

Conference committees, standing committees, officers and rules were important parts of the formal structure of the House of Representatives. But there was more to the House.

The early House of Representatives was a lively and often confused place. One English visitor was amazed at some of the things that went on there. He heard some Representatives laughing and talking while others tried to hold serious discussions. He saw Representatives lounging, still wearing hats, with feet propped up on tables. He watched them sleep through important meetings. "This undoubtedly is a miserable place," the Englishman wrote. "Such a gang . . . makes one shudder."

The Englishman would have had more reason to

shudder if he had been in the House one day in 1798. On that occasion, Representatives Roger Griswold, of Lyme, Connecticut, and Matthew Lyon of Vermont began trading insults. Lyon and Griswold were old enemies in the House, but this exchange was worse than usual. It ended with Lyon aiming a stream of tobacco juice straight into Griswold's face.

Three days later, the two men continued their quarrel. In the middle of a debate, Griswold attacked Lyon (already nicknamed "the Spitting Lyon") with a hickory cane. Trying to fend off the blows that rained about his head and shoulders, Lyon staggered across the floor of the House. Reaching the fireplace, he grabbed a pair of tongs and struck back. As the men wrestled each other to the floor, their colleagues cheered them on.

This fight was not the only violence ever seen in the House. Fists were more common weapons than canes and tongs, though. Sometimes, several Representatives found themselves slugging it out together. Once a brawl ended in laughter as one Representative seized another's hair—and found he was holding a wig. "Hooray boys," he yelled, "I've got his scalp!"

Other House weapons were the brass spittoons provided for tobacco-chewing Representatives. During one lengthy speech, a group of Representatives burst into the chamber, picked up the spittoons, and began

Fireplace tongs and a hickory cane were the weapons in the famous battle between Representatives Lyon and Griswold. A cartoonist drew this picture of the fight in the year it took place—1798.

beating them and tossing them about. This so alarmed the Representative who was speaking that he stopped talking and dropped back into his seat.

Guns, too, have appeared in the House. A member from Louisiana once cocked a pistol at a member from Ohio and threatened to shoot him. One Speaker of the

House wore a gun as he presided over meetings. The Speaker feared the House planned to elect someone to replace him. He intended to cling to his office—by force if necessary.

Other members of the House, although not violent, have been eccentric. John Randolph of Virginia served in the House during the early 1800s. He had a hot temper which sometimes came out while he was debating. Randolph also had the habit of arriving at the House in riding boots and spurs and carrying a whip. And he often brought his hunting dog to lie at his side. Another Representative, Tennessee's Davy Crockett, enjoyed letting the House know that he was a real frontiersman. He spoke and acted more roughly around the other Representatives than he did with his friends.

Crockett served in the House during the 1830s. By then, the United States was different than it had been in 1789. The big cities of the East were getting bigger. Pioneers were pushing westward, over the Great Plains, across the Rocky Mountains, and on to California. The country's population was growing. In 1790, it had been four million. In 1830, it was more than twelve million.

Since House membership was based on population, that meant the House was getting larger, too. In 1790, there were sixty-five Representatives. Seven years later, there were a hundred and five and by

1830, two hundred and forty-two. Membership rose until 1910. In that year, there were four hundred and thirty-five Representatives, and the House voted to "freeze" the membership at that number. Today, there are still four hundred and thirty-five Representatives, although the population of the country has more than doubled since 1910.

As the House grew, it changed. In its early days, House debates were almost unlimited. Any member could speak as long as he wished on any matter.

The House of Representatives has grown from 65 members in 1789 to 435 members today. Here, all 435 rise to take their oath of office on January 4, 1977. Thomas O'Neill, Jr. of Massachusetts is Speaker.

Debates in the early House were lively affairs. This one must have delighted the visitors in the gallery above the House floor. At least four Representatives are trying to shout each other down as the Speaker uses his gavel in an effort to quiet them.

Gradually, though, the Representatives realized that they must change their rules. If each member were allowed to speak as long as he liked, the House would not have the time to pass any bills at all. So in 1841, the Representatives agreed that no speech could last longer than one hour.

But this limit was not strict enough. If all two hundred and forty-four members of the House spoke for an hour apiece, a debate might have dragged on for two hundred and forty-four hours. At that rate, it could have taken months to pass a bill. And a few years later, the Representatives learned that even stricter limits were not enough. For while the House was cutting down the amount of time each Representative could speak, the number of Representatives in the House was going up. Debates were lasting as long as ever.

Finally, in 1890, Speaker of the House Thomas Reed of Maine decided to deal with the problem in a different way. Reed asked the House to agree to rules

Thomas Reed of Maine was one of the House's most powerful Speakers. The changes in rules that he forced through the House helped cut long, pointless debates.

that would speed up meetings. For example, he wanted the Speaker to take votes more quickly. He also wanted to give the Speaker the power to cut off long, pointless debates.

This request created an uproar among Reed's enemies in the House. They were against any rules that would give more power to Speaker Reed. So when the House was about to vote on the new rules, Reed's enemies began leaving the chamber. They knew that if enough of them left, there would be no quorum. Then there could be no vote.

Watching from the Speaker's chair, Reed realized what was happening. Quickly, he ordered the House doors locked. Reed's angry foes hid under desks, behind screens—anywhere at all to keep from being counted.

It didn't work. Reed's supporters dragged them out and counted them. The vote was taken. Reed won and the new rules went into effect that week.

For a time, the rules did speed up law-making in the House. But they gave great power to the Speaker, and that made a new problem. Now, a Speaker could use the rules to cut off all debate on any bill that he did not like. Even if most of the Representatives favored a bill, the Speaker could single-handedly defeat it.

By 1910, the House decided it was time to change the rules again. This time, the Representatives took power away from the Speaker and gave it to the Rules Committee. Now the Rules Committee would decide when, and whether, a bill would be debated. It was the Rules Committee, not the Speaker, that held the power to keep bills from being voted on. And the Rules Committee used its power to block many important bills.

So the House once more changed its rules. In 1975, the Representatives voted to take power from the Rules Committee and give it back to the Speaker. They expect the Speaker to use that power to force the House to act promptly on needed bills. If Speakers don't cooperate, the House can always change its rules again.

This may seem strange. If you're playing a game and things start to go badly for your team, you can't just make up new rules. But when enough Representatives think things are going badly, they do change the rules. Is that fair?

It is fair. It's necessary, too. The job of the House is passing bills: bills having to do with education, taxes, jobs, other nations, health and safety, business, conservation, crime, and so on. If House rules keep needed bills from passing, then those rules must be changed.

Of course, passing bills is not the job of the House of Representatives alone. It's a job the House shares with the other part of Congress—the Senate.

Chapter **4**

THE SENATE

The Senators looked happily around the room. The Senate chamber in New York's Federal Hall was small, less than half the size of the room set aside for the House of Representatives. That made sense, since the Senate had only about one-third as many members as the House.

Sunshine flooded in through high windows. Elaborately carved moldings set off doors, windows and ceiling. At the front of the room was a platform, draped with a crimson canopy, where the Senate officers would sit during meetings. Facing the platform were two semi-circular rows of tables and chairs for the Senators.

The room was lovely. But there was something else about it that pleased the Senators even more. The Senate chamber was on the second floor of Federal Hall, *above* the first-floor House chamber.

Compared to the House, the early Senate was a calm, dignified place. In this scene, Vice-president John Adams (on the rostrum) presides as Senate President, while the Secretary of the Senate takes notes at a table.

To many Senators, the fact that theirs was the Upper Chamber seemed more than just chance. They believed that under the Constitution, the Senate was more important than the House. As Senators, they thought, they would have more power and influence in the new government than the Representatives.

The Senators had some reason for feeling this way. For one thing, the Constitution set up slightly stricter qualifications for a Senator than for a Representative. Like a Representative, a Senator had to live in the state from which he was elected. But a Senator had to be at least thirty years old, to have been a citizen for at least nine years.

For another thing, the Constitution said that Senators and Representatives were to be elected in different ways. Representatives were chosen directly by the voters of their states and districts. True, not many people were allowed to vote in 1789. But those who could vote were able to cast a ballot for a member of the House.

But even white male voters were not allowed to vote for their Senators. The Constitution called for Senators to be selected by the government of each state. So Senators represented their *states*, not the *people* of their states. Many Senators felt that representing a state was a more important job than representing people. This system remained the same until 1913. In that year, the Constitution was amended to allow voters to choose their Senators as well as their Representatives.

Another reason that the Senators of 1789 felt superior to the Representatives was that the Constitution gave them certain responsibilities that members of the House did not share. For example, the Senate and the President had the joint power to make treaties and to choose people for many government jobs.

The Senate and the House were different in another way, too. The Senate was—and still is—a "continuing body." The House is not. Let's see what that means.

The United States holds Congressional elections in November of every even-numbered year. The first election took place in 1788. The Representatives who were elected then took office the next spring when the first session of the First Congress opened. They stayed in office during 1790, and the second session of the First Congress. When the next Congressional election was held, in November, 1790, all the seats in the House were up for election. The men elected, or re-elected, to those seats took office in 1791 at the beginning of the first session of the Second Congress. They served through 1792, and the second session of the Second Congress, and then all their seats were up for election once more.

Today, we still elect the House of Representatives in the same way. A new House took office in January,

1977, when the first session of the Ninety-fifth Congress opened. Its members remain in office during the second session a year later. When the Ninety-sixth Congress opens, in January, 1979, four hundred and thirty-five Representatives elected in 1978 will be starting new terms of office.

That doesn't happen in the Senate. Each Senator is elected to a six-year term. But the terms overlap each other. In each Congressional election, only one-third of the Senate seats are up for election. Two-thirds of the Senators continue in office. Therefore, an election makes less of a change in the Senate than in the House. It is possible for most—or even all—of the Representatives to be replaced in an election. But no matter what happens in an election, at least two-thirds of the Senators will keep their seats.

What with all these differences between the two houses of Congress, it's not too surprising that the first Senators thought of themselves as members of an Upper Chamber. But imagine their dismay when they discovered that the Representatives didn't think of themselves as part of a Lower Chamber! Right from the start, the Representatives made it plain they felt fully equal to the Senators. What's more, they were determined to turn this belief into fact. One of their first chances to do so came over the matter of Congressional salaries.

The Constitution says that members of Congress

may set their own salaries, and in 1789, the House suggested that each Congressman get a salary of six dollars a day, plus a small travel allowance. The Senate agreed that such a salary was fine—for a Representative. But a Senator deserved more. The Senators from South Carolina, Pierce Butler and Ralph Izard, spoke strongly on this point. Said Butler, "A member of the Senate should not only have a handsome income, but should spend it all." Izard warned that on six dollars a day, Senators would have to live in "holes and corners." In the end, though, the Senate gave in and accepted the idea of equal salaries.

The House and Senate also had to decide how to exchange official messages, such as requests for conference committee meetings. The Senate suggested that its messages to the House could be carried by a paid employee of the Senate. Upon entering and leaving the House, he would bow to the Speaker. However, messages from the House to the Senate would be delivered by two members of the House. These two Representatives would have to bow to the officers of the Senate.

The House turned this plan down at once. The Representatives had no intention of humbling themselves before the Senate. They demanded—and got— the Senate's agreement to exchange messages by way of paid employees of *both* houses.

The Senate also considered more important business, such as choosing officers. Under the Constitution, the Vice-president of the United States serves as the President of the Senate. He presides over meetings, and whenever a Senate vote ends in a tie, he casts a vote to break the tie.

The Senators knew, though, that a Vice-president might not always be on hand to run Senate meetings. The President might have other work for him to do. So the Senators chose one of their number to be President pro tempore—temporary president of the Senate. His job was to act as Senate President when the Vice-president was busy elsewhere.

The President pro tempore is just one Senate officer. The Senators chose others, including a secretary and doorkeepers. They agreed with the Representatives to invite clergymen of different faiths to act as chaplains for Congress.

Like the Representatives, the Senators decided to rely upon committees to help them in their work. As in the House, the number of committees has grown over the years. By 1977, there were nineteen committees and one hundred subcommittees.

The first Senators also knew they needed rules, and they adopted a set of twenty. According to one rule, Senators could not talk or read while a debate was going on. Another said that, on the Senate floor, no Senator might address a fellow Senator as "you." Instead, Senators referred to each other as "my

learned colleague," or "the honorable Senator from so-and-so."

With rules like these, the Senate was a much calmer and quieter place than the House. Senate visitors spoke of that body's "most delightful silence," and praised the Senators' "most beautiful order, gravity and personal dignity."

Opposite: This engraving shows the Senate Foreign Relations Committee at work more than a hundred years ago. This committee, one of the most important in the Senate, deals with matters having to do with the United States and other countries.

Below: The Senate Foreign Relations Committee at work today. Microphones and TV cameras lend a modern touch, but the committee's job is the same now as it has been in the past. Here, members question an expert witness about American dealings in Africa.

During the new government's first years, the rough-and-tumble House was the more exciting branch of Congress. House debates were livelier than those in the Senate. The Representatives seemed to brim over with ideas about how to make the government work. Many members of Congress thought being a Representative was better than being a Senator. Ambitious James Madison had no wish to leave the Lower Chamber. As a young man who wanted to get ahead in government, he said, he could not afford to become a Senator.

But by 1820, the situation was changing. The House was larger. Debates took longer. They were less lively. Representatives were not coming up with so many ideas for solving the country's problems, and by 1820, the country was facing serious problems.

The problems centered around slavery, the way of life in the South. Most white Southerners defended the system. They said they needed slaves to work in their homes and to labor on their huge cotton and tobacco plantations.

In the North, many people opposed slavery. They thought it inhuman, and hoped that someday Congress would abolish it around the country. Until that happened, they were anxious to keep slavery from spreading into the new states that were joining the Union.

The quarrel between North and South grew bitter. People began to talk of splitting the United States into two separate countries—one with slavery and one without.

Should the Union be allowed to fall apart? People who said "no," looked to Congress for a way to keep it together. The House was getting too large, its debates too slow, to work out a plan. The Senate, with just forty-four members, was different. Forty-four Senators could come up with a variety of ideas and suggestions. At the same time, with only forty-four opinions to hear, the Senators could keep their debates brisk and to the point. It seemed to be up to the Senate to keep the Union from breaking apart.

For forty years, the Senate did just that. Starting in 1820, the Senate worked out—and both houses of Congress passed—a series of compromise bills. Each provided for admitting new states into the Union in pairs. Each time a "slave" state joined the Union, so did a "free" state.

The Senator who figured out the details of these compromises was Henry Clay of Kentucky. His efforts earned him the nickname "The Great Compromiser." Although Clay was a Southerner, he believed the Union as a whole was more important than any one part of the country. He was firmly opposed by a fellow Southerner, John C. Calhoun of South Carolina.

People called the strong, six-foot-two-inch Cal-houn the "cast iron man." Calhoun devoted his strength, and his great charm, to the South's cause. He believed Congress had no right to tell the people of a state whether or not they could own slaves.

Calhoun and Clay were two of the Senate's best-known members. A third was Daniel Webster of Mas-sachusetts. Webster hated slavery. He told the Senate that he would never vote in favor of it. In the deep musical voice that made him one of the Senate's greatest orators, he proclaimed: "I shall oppose all slavery . . . in all places, at all times . . . against all compromise."

But a time came when Webster went back on those words. In 1850, Clay came to him with a new compromise. It called for California to join the Union as a free state. In return, Northerners would send all runaway slaves back to their Southern owners.

Webster disliked the runaway slave part of the bill, but he felt he must support it anyway. If he did not, the bill might not pass. The Union might fall apart. Webster loved the Union even more than he hated slavery.

So Webster made his last great Senate speech in favor of the bill: "I wish to speak today," he said, "not as a Massachusetts man, nor as a Northern man, but as an American and a Member of the Senate of the

Henry Clay, the Great Compromiser, argues before the Senate in favor of his last compromise in 1850. The Senate agreed to Clay's bill, but eleven years later, the Civil War began.

United States . . . I speak for the preservation of the Union. Hear me for my cause . . ."

For three hours, the Senators listened to Daniel Webster. They voted in favor of the compromise. Once again, the Senate had bought time for the Union.

The Compromise of 1850 was Clay's last great

compromise. In 1861, the South declared itself a separate and independent nation. The North, led by President Abraham Lincoln, went to war against the South to try to force it back into the Union.

The Civil War lasted four years. In 1865, the North won. The Union was safe, and slavery was abolished.

With the war over, the Senate—and Congress as a whole—faced a new task: trying to get North and South to work together as a single nation again. Eventually, that task was accomplished, and Congress once more represented a united country.

5

MEETING CONGRESS

"... In the second Congressional district, the winner is Bob Brown. And in the race for governor ..." The television announcer's voice goes on, but the people in the crowded room drown it out with their cheers. These are the men and women who have worked, many of them for months, to get Bob Brown (an imaginary person) elected to the House of Representatives. Early on election night, they gathered to watch the returns come in. Now, with the word of victory, a celebration begins.

Bob Brown is celebrating, too. Proudly he thinks of his new title—Representative Bob Brown. He may be called Congressman Brown, as well. The word "Congressman" can mean either a Senator or a Representative, and that's the way it's used in this book. But in newspapers or on radio or TV, "Congressman" usually refers to a member of the House. A Senator is generally called "Senator."

Brown decided to become a candidate about a year ago. Since then, he's campaigned hard—traveling around his district, meeting voters, making speeches, appearing on radio and TV, and so on.

A candidate for Congress gets out to meet the voters. Perhaps he will tell the woman what he hopes to do in Congress to keep food prices from going up and up.

The campaign was tiring and expensive. It cost Brown thousands of dollars to win. Some of the money was his own. But much of it came from men and women who liked what Brown said he would do in Congress if he were elected.

For instance, Brown promised to vote for conservation and anti-pollution bills. He said he would support legislation to lower taxes for working people. And, most important to the voters in Brown's district, he promised to introduce a bill to provide new jobs for out-of-work men and women.

The people who contributed money to Brown's campaign—and those who voted for him—can't be sure that he will keep all his campaign promises. But by reading newspapers and watching TV, they can keep track of his actions in the House. If they think he's not keeping his promises, they will give their votes and their money to someone else in the next election.

Right after the election, Brown and his family begin to look for a house to buy or rent in Washington, D.C.. Of course, the Browns plan to keep their home back in their own state and district. They will vacation "back home" on weekends and when Congress has recessed, or is not in session. Nearly all members of Congress have two homes so they can be near their work, yet keep in touch with the people who elected them.

This Congressional candidate visited a school in Vassalboro, Maine, to explain his ideas. The students aren't yet old enough to vote, but they have lots of questions.

How do they afford two homes? Members of Congress earn $57,500 a year. This money comes from the United States government, not from the Congressmen's own state. In addition, a Congressman may earn some extra money by writing books or making speeches.

Another thing Brown does immediately after the election is choose a staff for his new Washington office. The people who work for a Congressman are very important, and he may use them in many ways. Staff members read mail, type letters, and file papers. They

Surrounded by piles of books and papers, a Congressman discusses important business with two staff members. A Congressman's staff helps write speeches, research legislation, answer mail, and much more.

write speeches which the Congressman will deliver on the floor of Congress. They help him decide which bills to support. Some of their time is spent in doing research at the Library of Congress. This library, which is open to all Americans, contains seventy-five million books, magazines, photos, and other items.

Besides his Washington staff, a Congressman usually has people working for him in one or more offices back home. If you live in or near a city, you can probably find your Congressmen's offices listed in the telephone book. The people in these offices answer questions, listen to complaints, and let the Congressman know how his constituents are thinking and feeling.

As a member of the House, Brown may hire a staff of eighteen men and women. The money to pay them—about $250,000 a year—also comes from the federal government. However, it's different for a Senator. The size of his staff, and the amount he pays them, depend partly on how important he is. The chairman of an important Senate committee has a larger staff than a newly elected Senator who is not yet powerful in Congress.

Now that his staff is all set to begin work, Brown is ready to move to Washington and start his job as a Representative. One of his first actions is helping to select House officers for the coming two years.

Selecting officers is a matter of politics. There are

two major political parties in Congress—and in the United States. They are the Republican Party and the Democratic Party. Usually, members of each party vote along party lines. They agree with each other and disagree with members of the other party. If most Republicans are in favor of a particular bill, most Democrats will probably be against it. Of course, that isn't always true. If a Republican introduces a bill that will help farmers, members of both parties from farming areas will probably support the bill. Members of both parties from non-farming areas might oppose it. Or a member of either party may strongly dislike the bill his party supports. He may go against his party and refuse to vote for its bill. But in general, Republicans and Democrats are on opposite sides of most bills.

Let's suppose that Brown is a Democrat. And let's suppose that in this Congress, there are more Democrats than Republicans in the House. That means the Democrats are the majority party. The Republicans are the minority party.

As a member of the majority party, Brown will have the chance to help choose the House's chief officer—the Speaker. (Since the Speaker is elected by a majority of votes, he is naturally a member of the majority party.) The Speaker is chosen at a Democratic Party *caucus*—a private meeting of all the Democrats in the House.

After voting for the Speaker, Brown takes part in

choosing other party leaders, such as the majority leader and the majority whip. A party *whip* is a member who is chosen in caucus to round up all party members when a bill that is important to the party is

about to be voted on. The leader and the whip are responsible for making sure that the Democrats work closely together to pass the bills their party favors.

At a separate Republican meeting, the Republicans choose a minority leader and whip. In the Senate, too, Republicans and Democrats choose majority and minority leaders and whips. The majority party in the Senate also picks the President pro tempore of the Senate.

The President pro tempore, the Speaker of the House, and the party leaders are Senators and Representatives who have served in Congress for years. Brown knows he has no chance of being elected to such an office. But as a freshman, or first term Representative, he will be chosen to serve on several committees and subcommittees.

Brown hopes that one of his committees will be the Armed Services committee. It is a powerful and important committee. Besides, Brown is interested in military affairs. Like all freshman Congressmen, he goes to the leaders of his political party in Congress to

Senate Majority Leader Robert Byrd, Democrat of Virginia (right) and Senate Minority Leader Howard Baker, Republican of Tennessee (left) phone the President to inform him that the Senate is going into session and is ready to transact the legislative business of the country. According to law, the President has to be so informed.

Before a committee hearing, a Congressman may speak privately with some of the witnesses. During the hearing itself, questions and answers will be more formal.

try to get an appointment to each committee of which he'd like to be a member.

Brown's introduction to Congress involves more than politics and committee appointments. It means becoming familiar with Congress's home—the Capitol.

Brown finds the Senate chamber an impressive room. At the front is a rostrum at which the Senate officers are seated. Facing it are four curved rows of desks and chairs. They are divided by an aisle down the middle. Each Senator has his own seat. Democratic Senators sit on the right of the aisle. Republicans sit on the left. Along the sides of the chamber, doors lead to smaller rooms—the lobbies and cloakrooms—where Senators can meet for informal chats. Above the doors are galleries where visitors to the Senate are seated.

But striking as the Senate chamber is, Brown is more interested in the room where the House of Representatives meets. Here, too, curved rows of seats face a rostrum. As in the Senate, Democrats and Republicans are separated by an aisle. But House members have no desks; with four hundred and thirty-five members, the chamber is too small. And Brown will not have his own special seat as he would if he were a Senator. He may sit anywhere on the Democratic side of the House. The room is circled by a visitors gallery, beneath which are doors that lead to the outer rooms.

Brown leaves the House chamber satisfied. He is eager to start the day-to-day work of being a Representative.

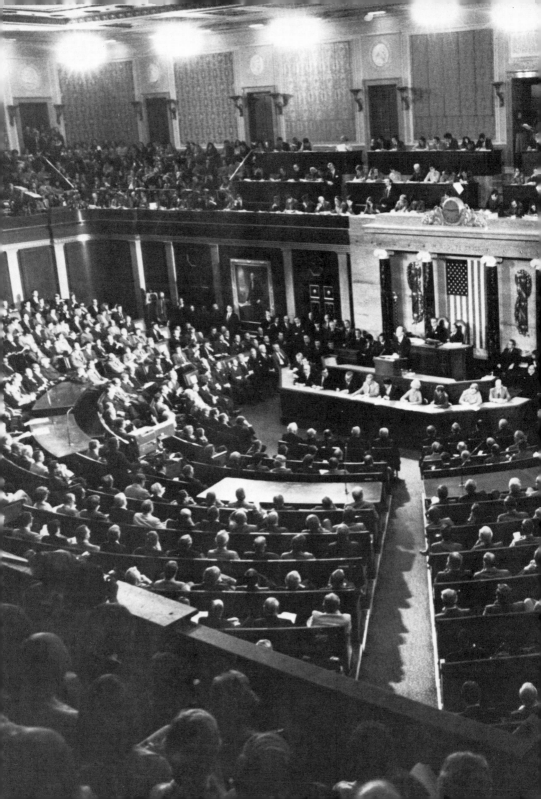

When the President makes his State of the Union Address each January, Senators and Representatives meet in a Joint Session in the large House chamber. But during ordinary meetings, the House chamber is not this full. The seats of Democrats and Republicans are separated by an aisle. The Speaker's chair is at the front of the room, and visitors sit in the gallery 15 feet above the floor.

Chapter 6

IN CONGRESS

Brown reaches his office in one of Capitol Hill's five large office buildings at about nine o'clock each morning. There, he meets with his staff, glances at important mail, and catches up on the news. He's careful to read news items from his own state as well as news from Washington. Keeping up with local affairs is one way he stays in touch with the people who elected him.

Next, Brown checks his appointments for the day. A desk calendar tells him he has four committee meetings scheduled for ten o'clock this morning. Such a conflict is common. Brown belongs to eight different committees and subcommittees, and usually several of them meet at the same time. He often has to decide which meetings to go to and which to skip. When he must miss a meeting, he asks a member of his staff to go in his place and let him know what went on.

72

After deciding which staff members will cover the meetings he can't get to, Brown sets off for the meeting that he will attend. To save time, he takes the Capitol subway. The subway's small cars carry him speedily and without charge from his building to the one where the meeting is being held.

At this meeting, committee members will consider a bill that calls for the federal government to spend more money on public schools. The committee

Some members are absent, but the committee is about to begin work. The chairwoman sits in the center. The man at lower left will record what is said.

is divided over the bill: some support it, but others do not. To give all the members a chance to learn more about how much money the public schools need, the committee chairman has invited education experts to appear. Members will listen to the experts and question them. At a later meeting, they will discuss what they have learned today, and decide whether to report the bill favorably to the House, or to "kill" it.

When the meeting ends, Brown checks his watch. It's almost time for lunch. But first, he takes the subway to the Capitol. In his briefcase is a bill he wants to introduce in Congress.

Since Brown is a member of the House, he can introduce his bill quickly and easily. He simply places it, neatly typed on an official paper, in the hopper, a box on the Clerk's desk. One of the Clerk's assistants will give the bill a number. It will be printed up and copies given to all members of the House. A copy will appear in the Congressional Record. The Speaker will send the bill to a committee. Finally, it will be placed on a *calendar*—a list of bills in the order in which they will be debated or discussed.

But if Brown were a Senator, he would find that introducing a bill there is a more formal matter. When a Senator wants to introduce a bill, he rises to ask for recognition. He reads the title of the bill and says a few words about it. Then he hands it to a page—one of the teenage boys and girls who act as messengers in

In 1971, Congress broke a 182-year-old tradition of male pages only when it accepted four female pages. Here, two of them are sworn in. Pages attend school early in the day, then go to work in the House and Senate.

Congress—who carries the bill to the rostrum. Like a House bill, it gets a number, is printed, distributed, sent to committee, and placed on a calendar.

Now that he has introduced his bill, Brown goes to lunch. He hasn't far to go. He will be eating with some fellow members of the House in one of the two Capitol restaurants.

During lunch, Brown and his colleagues discuss a bill they introduced months ago. The bill—to cut down some types of pollution—is still in committee, and the Representatives are afraid it will be killed there. To try to prevent that, Brown says he plans to hold a news conference. He will tell reporters why he thinks the bill is important. The reporters will write and broadcast stories about the bill. If enough stories appear, Americans may begin urging their Congressmen to support the bill. That may help the bill get a favorable report from the committee.

As they leave the restaurant, the Congressmen run into a lobbyist. Lobbyists are men and women who work for various groups such as businesses, veterans' or consumers' organizations, conservation societies, the governments of other nations, and so on. A lobbyist tries to get Congressmen to vote for bills that favor the group he represents. Lobbyists get their name from the lobbies outside the House and Senate chambers where they often meet with Congressmen. About ten thousand lobbyists are registered with the Clerk of the House to work on Capitol Hill.

The lobbyist who stopped Brown represents an industry that pollutes the air. The industry's leaders oppose Brown's anti-pollution bill, and the lobbyist wants to explain why. But Brown has no time to listen. He's already late for an appointment with a reporter from a newspaper back home.

And he's going to be even later. Just as Brown reaches his office, a buzzer rings. That's a signal that Brown has to go to the House. Busy Congressmen rely on the buzzer system to let them know when they're needed at the Capitol. The system uses different signals to tell members when their house has convened, or opened, when they are needed to make up a quorum, and when a vote is about to be taken.

The signal that Brown has heard is for a vote. He knows the vote is on an act that the President vetoed and sent back to Congress. If two-thirds of the members of each house vote for the act, it will become law in spite of the veto.

Brown, and most other Democrats in Congress, hope the act *will* become law. For days, the House majority leader and whip have been working to get every Democrat in the House to vote for it. As Brown takes his seat, he waves at the whip to let him know he's here for the vote.

There are several ways a vote may be taken in the House. Often, it's *viva voce*—aloud. The Speaker calls for those who favor the measure to say "aye," and those who oppose it to say "nay." If the vote is lopsided, it's easy to tell which side has won. But if it's close, the House may demand a more exact way of counting the votes.

One way is by a teller vote. House members stand up and walk—"ayes" first, then "nays"—between two people called tellers who count each one. Another way of voting is by roll call. In a roll call vote, the Representatives answer "aye" or "nay" as their names are called. A roll call vote in the House takes close to an hour. In the Senate, it takes only five or ten minutes, so Senators vote by roll call more often than Representatives do. The Senate may vote *viva voce*, too.

Brown knows that since this is an important vote it will be by roll call. It's going to be close. Capitol Hill is gripped by excitement.

As each Congressman answers "aye" or "nay," his vote flashes onto a large "scoreboard" over the visitors' gallery. The "ayes" mount rapidly, and soon the result is clear. The House has overturned the veto. If the Senate votes the same way, the act will become law. This doesn't happen very often. In 1976, for example, President Gerald Ford vetoed twenty-four acts of Congress. Congress overturned four of those vetoes.

The vote over, Brown heads back to his office for the delayed meeting with the news reporter. The reporter has brought along a photographer, who snaps pictures as Brown explains what he's been doing in Congress and why. Tomorrow, his constituents will read his words, and have a chance to judge for themselves how well he's representing them in Congress.

It's been a long and busy day for Brown—and it's

not over yet. The President of the United States has invited Brown and the other Congressmen from his state to an evening reception at the White House. The reception is in honor of the governor of Brown's state, and Brown is looking forward to it. If he hurries, he'll have just enough time to get home and change into evening clothes before leaving for the White House. Even after the reception ends, Brown may go on working. Many Congressmen sit up long into the night, answering letters, reading reports, researching legislation.

This is the kind of schedule that many Representatives follow during the nine months of each year that Congress is in session.

Of course, no Congressman spends all his time working. Congressmen find time to spend with their families and friends. They play tennis or handball, or jog, or go to baseball games. They travel, sometimes on business, sometimes for pleasure. They go back home to visit with their constituents.

And soon, most of them begin to campaign for the next election.

Chapter 7

CONGRESS AND THE PRESIDENT

The Constitution says that the three branches of the federal government—executive, legislative, and judicial—are equal. Each branch checks and balances the other two.

Really, though, it's not that simple. Some Presidents are strong. Others are weak. Some Congresses accomplish more than others. Sometimes judges make decisions that lead to changes in the laws of the land, and at other times they do not. So the balance among the three branches is never exact. Sometimes one branch is stronger. Sometimes another.

But over our country's history, one thing has been true. Presidents have tended to become stronger. Congress has tended to become weaker.

Why? One reason is Congress's size. There are five hundred and thirty-five men and women in Congress. That's too many people to act quickly in an emergency.

Suppose a fierce blizzard strikes the Midwest. Motorists are stranded. Towns are cut off without fuel supplies. People can't get food. The Midwest needs help—at once.

How fast can Congress act? Congressmen from the Midwest are ready to rush help—money, snow-plows, food, and fuel—to their states. Congressmen from other parts of the country are in less of a hurry. Are conditions really that bad in the blizzard states? They want time to find out. What kind of help is needed most? Food? Fuel? The Congressmen start to argue. Five hundred and thirty-five individuals have opinions that must be heard. Committees begin to meet. Time passes.

How fast can the President act? He calls in three or four advisors and asks them to suggest the best ways to help the people of the Midwest. Within hours, a plan has been set up and help is on the way.

Obviously, the President—a single person—can handle the blizzard emergency more quickly than Congress. Over the years, Presidents have dealt speedily with many different kinds of emergencies. Gradually, Americans have come to expect the President, not Congress, to act when action is needed. Many people expect strong Presidential leadership even when that leadership goes against the Constitution.

For example, the Constitution gives Congress—not the President—the power to declare war. But some

Presidents have led the United States into war without even asking Congress for permission. The Presidents explain it this way:

If another country attacks or threatens the United States, we can't wait for a committee to investigate. We can't let Americans be killed while a roll call vote is going on. We must strike back at once.

For years, most Americans seemed to agree. But by the early 1970s, some had changed their minds. Maybe we should take time for a quick investigation, they suggested. An investigation might show that the threat isn't really very serious. Perhaps the United States doesn't really have to strike back at all. Delay might *save* lives.

In 1973, Congress tried to take back part of its Constitutional power to declare war. It passed a bill— the War Powers Act—that limits the President's ability to start wars. Under the law, a President may send troops into action in an emergency. But within sixty days, Congress must vote whether or not the troops should go on fighting.

Another power that Congress has been losing is the power to decide when and how the United States will spend money. Under the Constitution, when Congress passes a bill that calls for spending money, Congress also determines how much may be spent. For instance, in 1972, Congress decided to try to clean up some of the nation's polluted rivers. Congress voted to spend nearly thirty billion dollars on the anti-pollution effort.

But that isn't the end of the story. The President thought that thirty billion dollars was too much. He *impounded* the funds, refusing to allow them to be used as Congress wished.

The impoundment angered many Congressmen, and two years later, they passed a bill that forbids a President to impound money that Congress has voted to spend. This act is the Congressional Budget and Impoundment Control Act. Besides outlawing impoundments, the act aims to make sure that Congress keeps its right to decide how to spend federal money.

Passing the Impoundment Act and the War Powers Act were signs that Congress was trying to get back into balance with the President. As it turned out, these acts were just the beginning. In 1974, Congress was facing a far more drastic action against a President. That action was impeachment, and the President was Richard M. Nixon.

The Constitution gives the House the right to impeach a President—to accuse him of committing crimes while in office. If a majority of Representatives vote to impeach a President, he goes on trial in the Senate. If two-thirds of the Senators vote guilty, the President is removed from office.

Only once before had Congress considered forcing a President from office. In February, 1868, the

From February to May, 1868, the country waited to learn the fate of President Andrew Johnson. Impeached by the House, Johnson was on trial in the Senate. Finally Johnson, the only American President ever impeached, was found innocent.

Andrew Johnson

House impeached President Andrew Johnson. The next month, Johnson went on trial in the Senate. He was found "not guilty" by just one vote. Later, many people argued that Johnson was not really impeached for a crime, but rather because Republicans in Congress disagreed with the Democratic President's political ideas.

In Nixon's case, though, the President *was* accused of committing crimes. People said President Nixon had ordered lawmen to listen in on the telephone conversations of thousands of Americans. They said the President had set spies on news reporters, politicians, writers, and others.

Congress knew it was against the law for the government to spy on American citizens. If the President had ordered such activities, he had committed crimes. He ought to be impeached and tried.

Were the accusations true? To find out, the House told its Judiciary Committee, which deals with matters of the law, to investigate.

The investigation lasted six months. Committee members and their staffs questioned thousands of people. They read long reports about the people Nixon met and talked with, and about the orders he gave them. Finally, a majority of committee members agreed: Nixon had committed at least some of the crimes he was accused of. The committee voted to

Representatives Barbara Jordan of Texas and Charles Rangel of New York served on the House Judiciary Committee while it investigated the possible impeachment of President Richard Nixon in 1974. Here, the two look over a copy of the Constitution.

recommend that the House of Representatives impeach the President.

The House never did so, however. On August 5, 1974, Nixon made more of his records public. Millions of Americans—and nearly every member of Congress—believed these records contained definite proof that Nixon was guilty of law-breaking. Four days later, President Nixon resigned from office. Vice-president Gerald Ford became President.

It was a sad moment for Congress. No Congressman enjoyed seeing an American President disgraced.

But it was a proud moment, too. Congress had had a responsibility to investigate criminal charges against a President. Congress had met that responsibility.

Now, many people, both in and out of Congress, said it was time for Congress to meet another responsibility: to take a close look at itself—and perhaps to make some changes.

8

CONGRESS
TODAY–AND TOMORROW

When the Ninety-fourth Congress opened, in January, 1975, its members did take a look at themselves. And they did make some changes.

One concerned the House Rules Committee. As we saw earlier, the Representatives agreed that the Rules Committee was using its great power to block action on too many good bills. Since it was up to the Rules Committee to decide when a bill could be debated, it hardly mattered whether or not a majority of the House supported a bill. Unless a majority of the Rules Committee supported it too, that bill had almost no chance of coming up for discussion and a vote.

So the House decided to give the Speaker the power to appoint a majority of the members of the Rules Committee. Naturally, the members the Speaker chooses will be men and women who agree with his ideas and who will support the bills he supports. That means the Rules Committee will probably speed up action on bills that the Speaker—and a majority of the House—favor.

Another change the House made was in the seniority system. Under that system, the chairman of each committee was the committee's senior member—the one who had been a member longest. The result: most committee chairmen were in their sixties or seventies. One was eighty-two years old. The seniority system did keep experienced Congressmen at the heads of important House committees. But it also kept young men and women from gaining power in Congress. Getting rid of the seniority system allows younger House members to be elected to chairmanships by their fellow committee members. It gives them more of a chance to come up with new ideas and new ways of dealing with the country's problems. In 1977, the Senate, too, began to move away from the seniority system.

The Senate was making other changes. One of them involved the filibuster.

The filibuster is a Senate tradition. Senate rules, like the early House rules, allowed unlimited debate. As we know, the Representatives had to place stricter and stricter limits on the time members could speak. In the smaller Senate, few limits have been needed. A Senator could speak almost as long as he wished or until his voice gave out. For years, it was nearly impossible to force a Senator to stop speaking or to "yield the floor."

Some Senators have used long speeches to keep a bill they dislike from being voted upon. They filibuster—talk and talk and talk and *talk*—until the rest of the Senators are so exhausted that they give up trying to pass the bill. That's what a filibuster is: a way for a few Senators to talk a bill to death.

But the Senate of the Ninety-fourth Congress changed that. They agreed that a vote by three-fifths of the Senators can force a filibustering Senator to yield the floor. Such a vote is called *cloture*.

Will changes in the rules—changes to do away with filibustering, the seniority system, and taking power from the Rules Committee—be enough to change Congress itself? Will the changes give us a Congress that is willing and able to help lead the country?

Senators and Representatives hope so. But others have doubts. They say Congress ought to make more basic changes. For example, Congress should take strong steps to make sure its members stick to high standards of honesty and good conduct.

The fact is that not all Congressmen are as honest and hard-working as our imaginary Congressman Bob Brown. Some are lazy. They skip more meetings and appointments than they have to. They go on luxurious vacations, and tell their constituents that they are taking "business trips." Some Congressmen are greedy.

Does Congress need to reform itself? Many Americans think so. Congressman Bruce Caputo (right) is a member of the House Ethics Committee, which helped write new rules of conduct for House members in 1977.

They spend much of their time making speeches—and being paid for making them—and skimp on their Congressional duties.

A few other Congressmen are dishonest. They avoid paying taxes. They let lobbyists pay for their vacations, or buy them expensive gifts. In return, they vote for whatever bills the lobbyists favor. They hire friends or relatives to work for them. But the friends or relatives, who are paid by the federal government, do little or no work.

In 1977, each house of Congress voted to adopt higher standards of conduct for their members. For example, they limited the amount of money a Congressman can earn by speech-making, and require that he let the public know how much money he makes each year.

But the new standards don't satisfy all Americans. Some argue that the standards are not really very high—not as high as the standards that most ordinary citizens have for themselves. And they point out that the new standards were just part of a "package" that Congress voted for.

What else was in the "package"? Along with the new standards, members of Congress voted to raise their pay from $42,500 to $57,500 a year. That's a very large raise, and Congress voted for it at a time when millions of people can't find any jobs at all. Many Americans think this action shows that members of

Congress are more interested in themselves than in the people they represent.

That idea makes people angry. And their anger isn't just at the Congressmen who are greedy or lazy or dishonest. They're angry at all Congressmen. Some have become so angry that they've "given up" on Congress. They don't bother to vote for either Senators or Representatives.

But getting this angry doesn't solve any problems. Refusing to vote for Congressmen doesn't mean that better people will start running for Congress. Saying that all Congressmen are lazy or dishonest won't make them work harder or be more honest.

We cannot improve Congress until we know more about it. We must learn how Congress is supposed to work, and what it is supposed to do, before we can try to make sure it is doing its job. And we must know about our Congressmen and women, who they are and what they are doing in Congress, before we can decide whether to give them our support—and our votes in the next election.

INDEX

94